TIM'S DIG

Derek Radford

CAMPBELL BOOKS

Tim's seat can turn round.
It faces the front when
he's driving…

...and faces the back when he's digging.

Tim is ready to start digging.

Strong legs keep
the digger steady…

…and the bucket at the front helps too.

Now Tim can dig a deep trench for the water pipes.

See how much soil Tim has dug out!

Tim scoops up the soil
in the digger's front bucket...

...and tips it into
a waiting lorry.

After a good day's work
Tim goes home…

...to a lovely hot bath!